MY FIRST NOVEL

A STORY PLOTTING WORKBOOK
for TWEENS & TEENS

TUCKER & PADGETT

First Edition 2025
ISBN: 979-8-9861629-9-7

Published in coordination by

Emerald Forest Books
Stanwood, WA 98292

First Fruit Press
Camano, WA 98282

My First Novel workbooks are available at a special discount when purchased in bulk for
schools, educators, and non-profit organizations. For more information, please email
orders@emeraldforestbooks.com

Printed in the United States of America
MyFirstNovelWorkbook.com

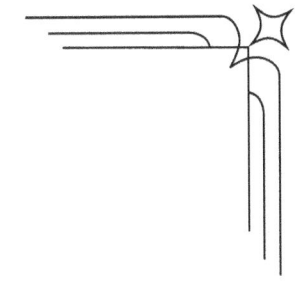

DEDICATION

To our younger selves:
Your stories deserve to be written. Keep going. Never give up.

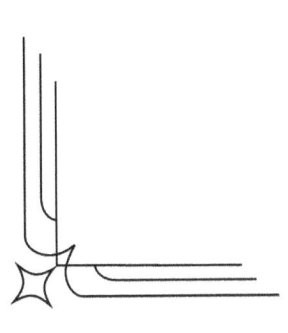
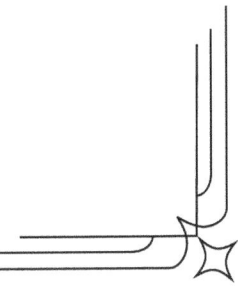

INTRODUCTION

Hi! We're Brittany and Brittany, two wild authors who fell in love with writing when we were young. Now, we're doing our best to help other young writers complete their first book!

Brittany Tucker:

Who am I? Not Spider-Man. I started my writing journey at seven years old with my attempts at *Power-Puff Girl*s fanfiction! Now, I'm a fantasy author writing what I love. When I was younger, I scoured the bookstores and libraries for books on writing craft. All I wanted was a guidebook to teach me the "rules" in a way that was practical and usable, not just some airy speech about finding my creativity. I have plenty of that! My hope is that this workbook will give you the information I so desperately sought when I was your age!

Brittany "Be" Padgett:

When I was a kid, I never imagined I could be a writer, let alone a published author. Reading and writing were my biggest struggles in school. It wasn't until I was ten that words and sounds finally clicked for me. I stopped hating reading and soon realized I adored it. And when you adore something, there's no portion control. I devoured books—multiple a day, like a starving monster set free. But reading them wasn't enough. I wanted to write them, dissect them, bring them to life. Back then, I didn't have anyone to teach me story structure or how to make exciting, memorable books. I gave it my best shot, but I yearned for guidance.

Why we wrote this workbook

This workbook is our gift to the world—to the younger versions of ourselves, who would have loved to have such advice and tools at their fingertips. Whether you're planning your first novel or your seventh, we hope this workbook helps you hone your skills and grow as a storyteller.

Have any questions? We love chatting and encouraging young writers. Email us: bepadgett@bepadgett.com or btucker@brittanytuckeryaauthor.com

CONTENTS

Check out what's inside!

SECTION 1
STORY ESSENTIALS

SECTION 2
BUILDING YOUR STORY

SECTION 3
HONING YOUR CRAFT

SECTION 4
RESOURCES & GUIDES

SECTION 5
ADDITIONAL SHEETS

SECTION 6
INDEX

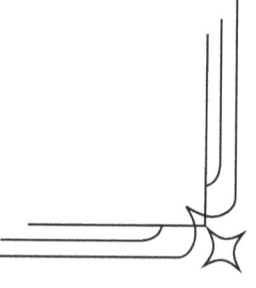

"Learn the rules like a
pro, so you can break
them like an artist."

Pablo Picasso

MY NOVEL AT-A-GLANCE

Title: _____

Genre: _____

Sub-genre: _____

Estimated Words: _____

Setting: _____

Theme: _____

Main Protagonist: _____

Main Antagonist: _____

Short Description: _____

_____

_____

_____

_____

_____

_____

_____

_____

_____

_____

Section 1:
STORY ESSENTIALS

WHAT IS A STORY?

A *STORY* is a **PERSON** with a **PROBLEM**.

The *PLOT* is how that **PERSON** solves the **PROBLEM**.

Think of your favorite books, shows, and movies. Would it exist if the *main character* didn't have insurmountable odds to overcome?

Keep in mind, a **problem** doesn't have to be the size of intergalactic war. It can be as simple as acing their school exams, or it can be as enormous as overthrowing an evil emperor.

The point is, in a **story**, one can't survive without the other. So, let's come up with some people and some problems.

WRITING TERM

A **character** is person in a story. A **main character** is called the **protagonist**!

WHAT IS YOUR PROBLEM?

How do you know if the **problem** you've chosen is good enough?
That's easy—just remember **P.U.P.**

P—PERSONAL

U—URGENT

P—PHYSICAL

Our Example Written Down:

Problem: *People disappearing from town.*

Personal: Protagonist's grandmother disappears.
Urgent: They must be found by the end of the week.
Physical: If they aren't found they will be gone forever.

Personal:

If your **problem** isn't personal to your **protagonist**, your reader won't have a reason to care about the events unfolding in your world.

Example: Are people mysteriously disappearing in the town you've created? Great. Now, make sure the missing people are important to your **protagonist**— friends, families, pets, etc. This will immediately hook the reader and help them build empathy toward your **protagonist**.

Urgent:

Now that your character has a personal **problem**, create a sense of urgency to resolve it.

Example: If your **protagonist's** family and friends have disappeared, create a limited time frame to find them. Time constraints create tension which keeps readers frantically turning the pages to find out what happens next.

Physical:

To keep the stakes high, make sure your **problem** has physical consequences to your **protagonist** if it's not resolved.

Example:
In epic fantasy, those physical consequences may be literal—death, injury, or maiming. In other genres, they might be smaller and internal—grief over losing a loved one, anxiety over a failed performance, or embarrassment of public failure. Your readers want to feel what your **protagonist** is feeling—so let them!

WHAT IS YOUR PROBLEM?

NOW YOU TRY!

Think about the **problem** in your story. Is it a small **problem**, like learning to tie your shoes? Or is it a big **problem**, like saving your family from a dragon? Use the space below to write out your problem, keeping P.U.P. in mind!

Write about your problem.

_____

_____

_____

How is this problem personal to your protagonist?

_____

_____

_____

_____

How is this problem urgent?

_____

_____

_____

_____

How is the problem physical to your character?

_____

_____

_____

BUILDING CHARACTER: WANTS VS. NEEDS

Think of something you really *want*.
Money for new shoes? The latest smartphone? To win the county triathlon?

Now think about something you *need*.
Friendship? A better relationship with your family?

You create **relatability** with your characters when they learn the difference between wants and needs. Most wants and needs are connected to bigger life lessons.

Here are some examples of how a want can be tied to a need:

WANTS

Attention

Win at every sport

Own the newest gadgets

Be popular

Get into the best college

Save their house

NEEDS

More self-esteem

Recognition for hard work

Appreciate what they have

Learn to be themselves

Accept disappointment

Understand what makes a home

NOW YOU TRY!

On the next page, make up a *want* and tie it to a *need* of the characters in your book.

BUILDING CHARACTER: WANTS VS. NEEDS

Make up a **want** and tie it to a **need** of the characters in your book. You can create as little or as many as you desire. Understanding what your character wants to achieve and needs to learn will help develop their path and support your theme.

Character's name: _____

Who are they in the story? (circle one)

       Protagonist   Antagonist   Side Character   Other: _____

What does this character want?

_____

_____

_____

What does this character *actually* need?

_____

_____

_____

_____

How will you connect what they want with what they need?

_____

_____

_____

_____

BUILDING CHARACTER: WANTS VS. NEEDS

Make up a **want** and tie them to a **need** of the characters in your book. You can create as little or as many as you desire. Understanding what your character wants to achieve and needs to learn will help develop their path and support your theme.

Character's name: _____

Who are they in the story? (circle one)

      Protagonist   Antagonist   Side Character   Other: _____

What does this character want?

_____

_____

_____

What does this character *actually* need?

_____

_____

_____

_____

How will you connect what they want with what they need?

_____

_____

_____

_____

CHARACTER SHEET

Draw or tape character
inspiration here.

First Name:_____

Last Name: _____

Physical Description: _____

_____

_____

_____

Age: _____

What does this character *want*? _____

What does this character *need*?_____

What are their flaws?_____
(*Check Flaws page 21 for ideas, pick no more than 2*)

What are their quirks?_____
(*Check Quirks Page 20 for ideas, pick no more than 2*)

Where do they live?_____

What do they do?_____

What do they love? _____

List things they hate: _____

List things they are good at: _____

List things they are bad at: _____

CHARACTER SHEET

What is their family like? _____

_____

_____

_____

_____

_____

_____

_____

_____

_____

What is their backstory? _____

_____

_____

_____

_____

_____

_____

_____

_____

_____

_____

_____

CHARACTER SHEET

Draw or tape character inspiration here.

First Name:_____

Last Name: _____

Physical Description: _____

_____

_____

_____

Age: _____

What does this character *want*? _____

What does this character *need*?_____

What are their flaws?_____
(*Check Flaws page 21 for ideas, pick no more than 2*)

What are their quirks?_____
(*Check Quirks Page 20 for ideas, pick no more than 2*)

Where do they live?_____

What do they do?_____

What do they love? _____

List things they hate: _____

List things they are good at: _____

List things they are bad at: _____

CHARACTER SHEET

What is their family like? _____

_____

_____

_____

_____

_____

_____

_____

What is their backstory? _____

_____

_____

_____

_____

_____

_____

_____

_____

_____

_____

CHARACTER SHEET

Draw or tape character
inspiration here.

First Name:_____

Last Name: _____

Physical Description: _____

_____

_____

_____

Age: _____

What does this character *want*? _____

What does this character *need*?_____

What are their flaws?_____
(*Check Flaws page 21 for ideas, pick no more than 2*)

What are their quirks?_____
(*Check Quirks Page 20 for ideas, pick no more than 2*)

Where do they live?_____

What do they do?_____

What do they love? _____

List things they hate: _____

List things they are good at: _____

List things they are bad at: _____

CHARACTER SHEET

What is their family like? _____

_____

_____

_____

_____

_____

_____

_____

_____

What is their backstory? _____

_____

_____

_____

_____

_____

_____

_____

_____

_____

_____

_____

CHARACTER SHEET

Draw or tape character inspiration here.

First Name:_____

Last Name: _____

Physical Description: _____

_____

_____

_____

Age: _____

What does this character *want*? _____

What does this character *need*?_____

What are their flaws?_____
(*Check Flaws page 21 for ideas, pick no more than 2*)

What are their quirks?_____
(*Check Quirks Page 20 for ideas, pick no more than 2*)

Where do they live?_____

What do they do?_____

What do they love? _____

List things they hate: _____

List things they are good at: _____

List things they are bad at: _____

CHARACTER SHEET

What is their family like? _____

_____

_____

_____

_____

_____

_____

_____

_____

What is their backstory? _____

_____

_____

_____

_____

_____

_____

_____

_____

_____

_____

_____

*Looking for more *Character Sheets*? Get additional sheets in the back of this workbook.*

QUIRKS SHEET

Quirks, everyone has them! They are unique behaviors, mannerisms, or qualities that make you you. In terms of your story, quirks are a great way to help readers relate and connect to your characters. Here are some ideas for quirks you can implement into your character's personality. *What would you add to the list?*

Only wears red shirts

Snorts when laughing

Scared of birds

Chews on their pencils

Only eats green apples

Nail biting

Wears sandals in the snow

Repeats the same phrase

Collects stamps

Avid crocheter

Talks to their pets like their humans

Doesn't like getting their hands sticky

Has an allergy

Can sleep anywhere

Clumsy

Fidgets when stressed

Can't stand wrinkles in clothes

Unmanageable hair

Hiccups when nervous

Excellent whistler

A planner

Spontaneous

Makes up words

Doesn't like to sit with back to the door

Always hungry

Plays an instrument

Always late

Bounces on the heels

Loves conspiracies

Talks to themselves

Carries a water bottle everywhere

Horrible driver

Mischievous

FLAWS SHEET

Nobody is perfect. We are always learning and growing into better (*or worse! Villains maybe?*) people. Your characters shouldn't be perfect either. Give them internal struggles to overcome! Here's a list of some common personality struggles. ***Can you think of more?***

Defensive

Easily influenced

Hypocritical

Selfish

Self-conscious

Bad temper

Lies to spare others' feelings

Obnoxious

Impulsive

Jealous

Naive

Worries about what others think

Troubles making decisions

Afraid of everything

Anxious

Too competitive

Perfectionist

Stubborn

Prideful

Distrusting

Obsessive

Arrogant

Insensitive

Sore loser

Rude

Forgetful

Sneaky

Nosy

Lazy

Oblivious

Poor listener

Pessimist

Vengeful

Manipulative

Holds a grudge

Trouble maker

Vain

People pleaser

Judgmental

FAMILY TREE

Do you have characters who are related? Is your protagonist an heir to a fortune, a descendant from a legendary line of dragons, a kid with a lot of siblings? Then use this family tree tool to remind you how your characters are connected to each other. **Draw lines between boxes to indicated how each person is related. Use as many boxes as you need.**

Name:

Born:_____
Note:_____

Name:

Born:_____
Note:_____

Name:

Born:_____
Note:_____

Name:

Born:_____
Note:_____

Name:

Born:_____
Note:_____

Name:

Born:_____
Note:_____

Name:

Born:_____
Note:_____

Name:

Born:_____
Note:_____

Name:

Born:_____
Note:_____

Name:

Born:_____
Note:_____

Name:

Born:_____
Note:_____

Name:

Born:_____
Note:_____

Name:

Born:_____
Note:_____

Name:

Born:_____
Note:_____

Name:

Born:_____
Note:_____

Name:

Born:_____
Note:_____

Name:

Born:_____
Note:_____

Name:

Born:_____
Note:_____

Name:

Born:_____
Note:_____

Name:

Born:_____
Note:_____

Name:

Born:_____
Note:_____

Family Name

SETTING

Also called, *world building.* Building a **setting** can often be a writer's favorite part of the process! Whether you're writing science fiction set on Mars, or a small-town drama, a detailed world is essential for immersing a reader into your setting. This can feel intimidating, but if you break it down into smaller chunks, it becomes much less overwhelming!

Here are a few places to start:

WRITING TERM

A **setting** is the time and place the story happens.

Time Period:
Even if your story is fantasy or sci-fi, it's important to have an idea of era. Is it far future, with massive spaceships and battle droids, or set in the style of medieval England? This will help you get an idea of what technology and tools are available to your characters.

Landscape:
Is your world set in an underwater city? A desert where water is scarce? A jungle, where predators are lurking around every corner? Finding the landscape you want will allow you to understand what's important for your character, whether it be a glass of water or bug spray to defend themselves from mosquitos.

Government:
This one might seem odd, but your readers need to know who's making the rules in your world. Whether it be a weathered king, a school principle, or an evil overlord, decide the social hierarchy your character has to navigate.

NOW YOU TRY!
On the next page, we will plan out our **setting** and start building the ideas of the world our characters will be in.

WHERE IS YOUR STORY?

Think about your problem in your setting. This is a great place to put down all your notes about your world. You can always come back and add more!

Where is your story primarily set? _____

(*Outer space, Washington State, fantasy forest, under water.*)

Name of your world: (*Could be real or made up.*)

_____

What is the time period(s)?_____

_____

_____

_____

Where does your story start?

_____

_____

_____

Describe the landscape: _____

_____

_____

_____

_____

_____

WHERE IS YOUR STORY?

What is the government system like? (*It can be real or made up.*)

_____

_____

_____

_____

Who is in charge? (*A president, a king, a queen, etc.*)

_____

What are some of the big rules people have to follow in your setting?

_____

_____

_____

_____

What currency do they use? (*dollars, coins, stardust, etc.*) _____

Additional setting notes:

_____

_____

_____

_____

WHERE IS YOUR STORY?

Sometimes our stories have more than one **setting**. Use these pages to fill as little or as many setting details you need.

Where is your story primarily set? _____

(Outer space, Washington State, fantasy forest, under water.)

Name of your world: *(Could be real or made up.)*

_____

What is the time period(s)?_____

_____

_____

_____

Where does this part of your story start?

_____

_____

_____

Describe the landscape: _____

_____

_____

_____

_____

_____

WHERE IS YOUR STORY?

What is the government system like? (*It can be real or made up.*)

_____

_____

_____

_____

_____

Who is in charge? (*A president, a king, a queen, etc.*)

_____

What are some of the big rules people have to follow in your setting?

_____

_____

_____

_____

What currency do they use? (*dollars, coins, stardust, etc.*) _____

Additional setting notes:

_____

_____

_____

_____

*Looking for more *Setting Sheets*? Get additional sheets in the back of this workbook.*

DISCOVERING YOUR THEME

The **theme** of your book is the central message you're trying to convey about a topic that's important to you. It's a big-picture idea subtly woven throughout the story. You've already figured out the **problem** your character will face, a **theme is the deeper meaning that gives your story heart.**

Themes don't need to be preachy! You can use **foreshadowing** to convey your theme throughout your story by tailoring situations, characters, and events to show the reader the point you're trying to argue, rather than state it directly.

WRITING TERM

Foreshadowing are the hints in our stories for future events or messages.

In *A Christmas Carol* by Charles Dickens, Scrooge is visited by three spirits that help him see that he needs to make a change in his life. In the story, we see if Scrooge can really become a better person or if his decisions will doom him.

So, what is the theme of *A Christmas Carol*? Redemption, salvation, charity? All of those things!

How do you discover a theme for a story, you ask? Again, what are you passionate about? What issues push your buttons? Choose something you're passionate about and craft your story around that theme!

Let's brainstorm! What are some things you are passionate about?

Write as many as you like.

_____

_____

_____

_____

_____

_____

_____

THEME IDEAS

Need some ideas? Here are some themes that may get you thinking.

THEME IDEAS

Personal Growth/Identity

- Self-discovery
- Transformation
- Growing up
- Perseverance
- Empowerment
- Find your purpose

Relationships/Morality

- Friendship
- Family
- Love
- Compassion
- Forgiveness
- Honesty

Social Issues/Broader Ideas:

- Anti-bullying
- Environmental issues
- Freedom
- Revolution
- Balancing work
- Dreams

Conflict/Resilience

- Survival
- Fear
- Bravery
- Destiny
- Power
- Good vs. Evil

So, what is the difference between plot and theme? Sometimes people confuse plot with theme. Here is a good way to remember:

Theme is about a *central message* that is *subtly shared* through the story.

Plot is the *how* your character *solves the problem*.

WHAT IS AN ARC?

An **arc** is about structure and progression. **Arcs** can apply to the overall story, individual characters, and overarching themes. Paying attention to them ensures that the narrative feels complete and satisfying.

Things to Remember About Arcs!

- **Unresolved arcs can leave readers confused or unsatisfied**, like a TV show canceled on a cliffhanger. This is why it's crucial to ensure your main arcs are complete.

- **Does everyone in your story need an arc?** Probably not. Do our main characters need them? Absolutely.

 **Example:** Imagine if *Alice in Wonderland* ended without Alice leaving Wonderland. We'd have so many questions: What did her family think when she didn't come home? Would the Queen of Hearts still be chasing her?

- **Not all characters need an arc, but some might if they play a meaningful role**. This often happens when a character says something profound or takes an impactful action. A small resolution can be enough to tie up the loose ends.

 **Example:** We know that *A Christmas Carol* is about Ebenezer Scrooge. But if Charles Dickens didn't add the line, *"he did it all, and infinitely more; and to Tiny Tim, who did not die, he was a second father,"* we would never know if Tiny Tim survived after Scrooge's transformation.

Again, arcs don't have to be big.
If a supporting character mistrusts the protagonist, their arc could be completed by offering a helping hand at the last minute!

Section 2:
BUILDING YOUR STORY

THE FOUR ACT STRUCTURE

Story flow should be like a wave or the seasons. It should build to a breaking point (*winter to the peak of summer*) and then make a dramatic fall (*pun intended*) down to its conclusion (*summer back to winter*).

One way of creating these seasons in our stories is by following the **FOUR ACT STRUCTURE**.

It can be broken up visually like this:

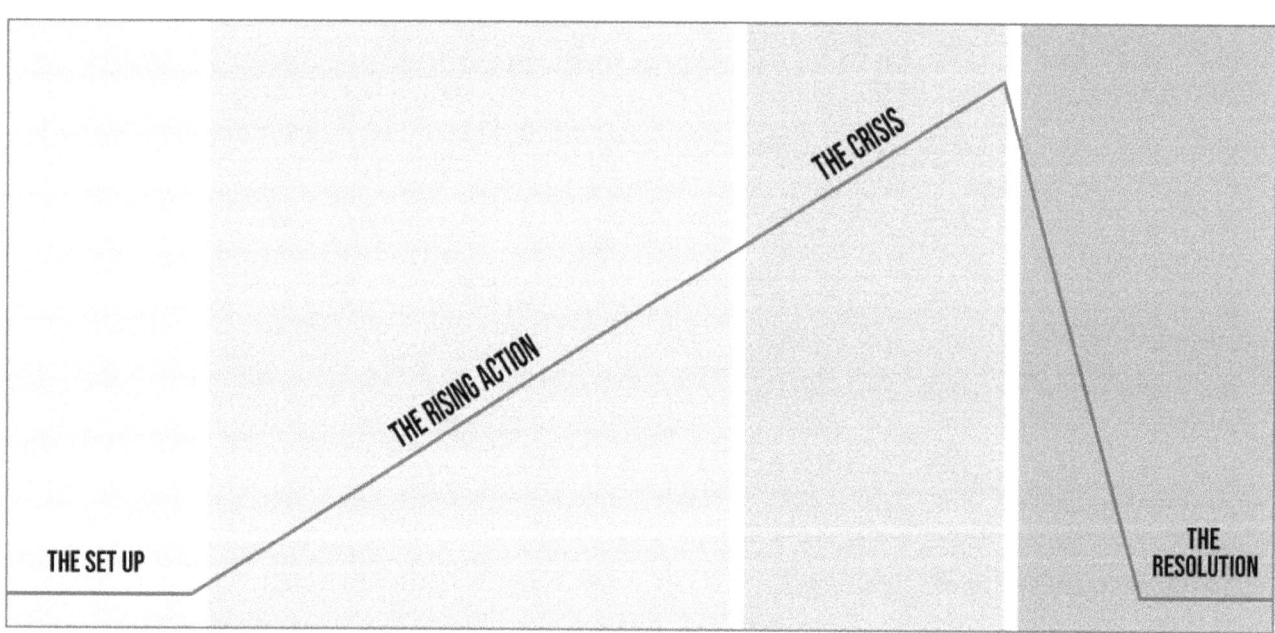

ACT 1 "THE SET UP"   **ACT 2** "THE RISING ACTION"   **ACT 3** "THE CRISIS"   **ACT 4** "THE RESOLUTION"

Even though there are many methods for writing story structure, this workbook focuses on the **FOUR ACT STRUCTURE**. It is a tried-and-true method and a great foundation for any writer.

The **FOUR ACT STRUCTURE** was designed to break story structure into smaller, more digestible parts: *the setup, the rising action, the crisis, and the resolution*. Each "Act" has its own plot points to break the big chunks into even smaller chunks. In the next part we will write out notes and ideas for those plot points.

ACT 1 - "THE SET UP"

ACT 1 needs to focus on introducing your characters and world to your reader. Does this **Act need to be boring?** Absolutely not! In this section you'll outline everything you need to prepare "The Set Up" for your Act 1. There are four major **plot points**!

WRITING TERM

Remember **plot** is *how* your character *solves* their problem. **Plot points** are the moments that *show* your character working to solve it.

PLOT POINTS
THE HOOK
FAMILIAR WORLD
THE INCITING EVENT
THE KEY EVENT

Here's something to remember--**the set up** should be between **10-20%** of your book!

NOW YOU TRY!

On the next pages, outline your Act 1 plot points. Put as little or as much detail as you want to prepare the set up for your story. You can always add more later.

ACT 1 - PLOT POINTS

THE HOOK

The **opening scene** *(also known as the opening image)* **of your story is the promise** you want to make to your reader. This is also where you'll give a hint of the story's **problem**. Write notes for your opening image. You're creating a scene that *shows* your protagonist or your story's world and "hints" at the **problem**.

Think about your opening image. How do you imagine your story starting?

_____

_____

_____

_____

Where does your hook take place? _____

How does this opening scene connect or hint at your problem?

_____

How will you make it feel like a hook and a promise of more to come?

_____

FAMILIAR WORLD

Now we switch over to **seeing your protagonist living their everyday life**. Show us who they are and how they feel about their current situations.

What does their everyday look like?

_____

_____

_____

_____

ACT 1 - PLOT POINTS

How do they feel about their familiar world? (Do they love their life? Are they miserable?)

_____

_____

_____

_____

THE INCITING EVENT

The inciting event or incident is **where your protagonist becomes aware that things are beginning to change**. Maybe their parents tell them they're moving. Maybe they get a message that aliens are about to blow up the planet. This event can be big or small but it needs to *show* us something is changing for the protagonist. Write your notes for your inciting event.

What will happen that will change your protagonist's world?

_____

_____

_____

_____

Additional notes for the inciting event:

_____

_____

_____

_____

_____

_____

ACT 1 - PLOT POINTS

THE KEY EVENT

What will make your protagonist become personally involved with the **Problem**? This is the turning point in which they start their journey. Now that the threat has been hinted at (or screamed from the rooftops) it's **time for your Protagonist to become personally involved with the Problem**. They may be reluctant to start their journey. Maybe they're excited. Either way, there's no going back!

How is your problem personal to your protagonist? (Remember P.U.P.? Look back at your notes.)

_____

What is your protagonist's attitude about the problem?

_____

Write notes about your key event that gets your character to start their journey:

_____

_____

_____

_____

_____

_____

CONGRATULATIONS!

You completed outlining for your Act 1. Now on to Act 2!

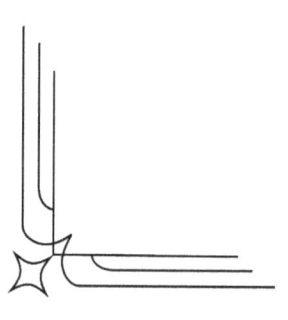

ACT 2 - "THE RISING ACTION"

ACT 2 of your story is all about building up the problem and **stakes** of your protagonist, including introducing any new characters and villains along the way. Here is what you need to prepare "The Rising Action" for Act 2.

PLOT POINTS
UNFAMILIAR WORLD
LEARNING THE ROPES
THE MIDPOINT

WRITING TERM

Stakes are what will happen if your character doesn't follow through with their journey. It's the consequences of their actions or choices.

The Rising Action will be the biggest section. About **40-60%** of your book happens in Act 2!

➡ NOW YOU TRY!

On the next pages, outline your Act 2 plot points. Put as little or as much detail as you want to prepare the set up for your story. You can always add more later.

ACT 2 - PLOT POINTS

UNFAMILIAR WORLD

We've seen your **protagonist** in their familiar world, and now their whole world has changed. They now are part of an unfamiliar world that can't be changed back. This is the time to throw them into the deep end—and they're going to feel like they're drowning. **Introduce them to terrifying new situations and people.** Let them make new friends or *enemies*.

The unfamiliar world needs to contrast with the protagonists familiar world. This is also a good place to introduce the ***Antagonist.***

WRITING TERM

An **antagonist** means "one that is in opposition." This doesn't have to be an opponent. It can be anything that opposes the goals of your protagonist.

What is your story's unfamiliar world? How does it *contrast* to the familiar world?

_____

_____

What/who is your antagonist? How do you see them being introduced?

_____

Write any additional ideas for this plot point:

_____

_____

_____

_____

_____

_____

_____

_____

ACT 2 - PLOT POINTS

LEARNING THE ROPES

Now that your character is treading water, it's time to see how cool they are. **This may be a series of scenes as you build up your team or character for what they will face ahead.** Sometimes it's investigating the clues, other times its learning new skills. Prepare your character for what will come ahead. **Help them feel prepared to be the potential hero.** Too bad this fresh burst of self-esteem won't last long.

What are some people, skills, clues that your character will need to learn or show in this section?

_____

_____

_____

Make notes for a series of scenes to introduce these things.

Scene 1:

_____

_____

_____

_____

_____

Scene 2:

_____

_____

_____

_____

_____

ACT 2 - PLOT POINTS

Scene 3:

_____

_____

_____

_____

_____

Need more? Check out the chapter outline notes at the end of this section.

THE MIDPOINT

The Midpoint, also called the **Reversal**, is when your **character comes close to achieving their first goal, only to realize what they wanted may not be what they needed.** Remember when we filled out that "want vs. need" sheet? It's time to review.

Write notes for scenes that will impact your character's journey both physically and emotionally. Break your character's heart. Make your readers cry. Tissues are optional.

How did your protagonist come to realize that their _want_ is different than their _need_? How does this impact their future decisions?

_____

_____

_____

_____

Things go from good to bad. What happens? Write notes for your reversal.

_____

_____

_____

_____

CONGRATULATIONS!

You completed outlining for your Act 2. Now on to Act 3!

ACT 3 - "THE CRISIS"

ACT 3 is about seeing the worst of the situation or **crisis** for your protagonist and other **characters**. Danger is closing in, **conflict** is rising, things were bad and now they are worse. Its about getting heroes to understand what they have to do to solve the **Problem**.

PLOT POINTS
WORDS OF WISDOM
THE WORST-CASE SCENARIO

WRITING TERM

Crisis is about intense dangers or trouble. It is usually external. **Conflict** is a disagreement. It can be an internal struggle or an opposing view.

The Crisis will be the lead up to your climax! It's only 10-20% of your book!

NOW YOU TRY!

On the next pages, outline your story's Act 3. Put as little or as much detail as you want to prepare the set up for your story. You can always add more later.

ACT 3 - PLOT POINTS

WORDS OF WISDOM

With your protagonist's plans in shambles, it's time for kind words from a friend or loved one to remind them why they embarked on this journey in the first place. It's time to become a hero. **Think about who or what can encourage your protagonist to continue on their journey.**

What does your protagonist need to hear or see to carry them through to the final battle?

_____

_____

_____

_____

How will they get this encouragement?

_____

_____

_____

Additional notes for Words of Wisdom:

_____

_____

_____

_____

_____

_____

ACT 3 - PLOT POINTS

THE WORST-CASE SCENARIO

Yes, I mean it. This is where you inflict the worst kind of pain on your protagonist. Their village is burned to the ground. They flunked out of football tryouts. Your character needs to hit rock bottom so they can prove their strength, whether internal or external.

Now is the time where everything is disastrous! No matter how many times they have tried it feels like they can't get ahead or success seems impossible.

Write down a few horrible things that make it harder for your character to solve their problem.

_____

_____

_____

_____

Now write down something that makes it even *worse*!

_____

_____

_____

_____

CONGRATULATIONS!

You completed outlining for your Act 3. Now on to the final Act!

ACT 4 - "THE RESOLUTION"

ACT 4 is where the **climax** of your story happens. It's time for the final battle and ending scenes. This usually happens in the last 20% of your story. Let's outline everything you need to complete "The Resolution" for your Act 4.

PLOT POINTS
THE FINAL BATTLE
THE CLOSING IMAGE

WRITING TERM

The **Climax** is the peak of the mountain in story structure. Its where the most exciting moment happens. The part that has you sitting at the edge of your chair.

The **Resolution** well . . . its the end. You're almost there. Whew!

NOW YOU TRY!

On the next pages, outline your story's Act 4. Put as little or as much detail as you want to prepare the set up for your story. You can always add more later.

ACT 4 - PLOT POINTS

THE FINAL BATTLE

It's time for the final show-down! Your character is pretty bruised and battered, but they charge forward anyway to meet their adversary on the field. The situation looks dire, but never fear—good always triumphs in the end. Even if it's not the triumph we expect.

The final battle is the *climax* of your story. It's where you will create the greatest **tension**.

WRITING TERM

Tension is what makes the reader turn the page. It's created through uncertainty, mystery, something sinister happening, and other ominous feelings.

How does the problem get solved?

_____

How can you increase the tension?

_____

Outline your notes for the final battle.

This happens:

_____

_____

Then this happens:

_____

_____

Then this happens!

_____

_____

Until finally....

_____

_____

ACT 4 - PLOT POINTS

THE CLOSING IMAGE

This scene should mirror of the **Opening Image.** It's time to **clean up any unresolved plot points and give your reader that closing image.** Where at first, we saw the problem building, now we see it defeated. Even if your character's original goals have changed, they're at peace with their choices. Even if their life is tougher now than it was before, they're ready to take on the responsibility, and be who they were always supposed to be: The Hero.

What feeling do you want to leave with the reader when they finish that last page?

_____

_____

_____

How do you imagine the closing image of your book?

_____

_____

_____

_____

Are there any mysteries still unsolved? If so, how will you resolve them or use them?

_____

_____

_____

_____

_____

CONGRATULATIONS!

You have a full outline for your book. You can use these notes and start writing out your chapters.

Want more planning? Check out the chapter outline section on the next page to really plan out the details!

CHAPTER OUTLINE NOTES

This is a space for you to plot out your chapters. Write notes that will help you through your writing process. No rules just anything you want to remember! Use as many or as few chapter notes as you need to tell your story.

CHAPTER 1 - TITLE (OPTIONAL): _____

Notes:_____

_____

_____

_____

_____

_____

_____

CHAPTER 2 - TITLE (OPTIONAL): _____

Notes:_____

_____

_____

_____

_____

_____

CHAPTER 3 - TITLE (OPTIONAL): _____

Notes:_____

_____

_____

_____

_____

_____

CHAPTER OUTLINE NOTES

CHAPTER 4 - TITLE (OPTIONAL): _____

Notes:_____

_____

_____

_____

_____

_____

_____

_____

CHAPTER 5 - TITLE (OPTIONAL): _____

Notes:_____

_____

_____

_____

_____

_____

_____

_____

CHAPTER 6 - TITLE (OPTIONAL): _____

Notes:_____

_____

_____

_____

_____

_____

_____

CHAPTER OUTLINE NOTES

CHAPTER 7 - TITLE (OPTIONAL): _____

Notes:_____

_____

_____

_____

_____

_____

_____

CHAPTER 8 - TITLE (OPTIONAL): _____

Notes:_____

_____

_____

_____

_____

_____

_____

CHAPTER 9 - TITLE (OPTIONAL): _____

Notes:_____

_____

_____

_____

_____

_____

_____

CHAPTER OUTLINE NOTES

CHAPTER 10 - TITLE (OPTIONAL): _____

Notes:_____

_____

_____

_____

_____

_____

_____

CHAPTER 11 - TITLE (OPTIONAL): _____

Notes:_____

_____

_____

_____

_____

_____

_____

CHAPTER 12 - TITLE (OPTIONAL): _____

Notes:_____

_____

_____

_____

_____

_____

_____

CHAPTER OUTLINE NOTES

CHAPTER 13 - TITLE (OPTIONAL): _____

Notes:_____

_____

_____

_____

_____

_____

_____

_____

CHAPTER 14 - TITLE (OPTIONAL): _____

Notes:_____

_____

_____

_____

_____

_____

_____

_____

CHAPTER 15 - TITLE (OPTIONAL): _____

Notes:_____

_____

_____

_____

_____

_____

CHAPTER OUTLINE NOTES

CHAPTER 16 - TITLE (OPTIONAL): _____

Notes:_____

_____

_____

_____

_____

_____

_____

CHAPTER 17 - TITLE (OPTIONAL): _____

Notes:_____

_____

_____

_____

_____

_____

_____

CHAPTER 18 - TITLE (OPTIONAL): _____

Notes:_____

_____

_____

_____

_____

_____

CHAPTER OUTLINE NOTES

CHAPTER 19 - TITLE (OPTIONAL): _____

Notes:_____

_____

_____

_____

_____

_____

_____

CHAPTER 20 - TITLE (OPTIONAL): _____

Notes:_____

_____

_____

_____

_____

_____

_____

CHAPTER 21 - TITLE (OPTIONAL): _____

Notes:_____

_____

_____

_____

_____

_____

CHAPTER OUTLINE NOTES

CHAPTER 22 - TITLE (OPTIONAL): _____

Notes:_____

_____

_____

_____

_____

_____

_____

CHAPTER 23 - TITLE (OPTIONAL): _____

Notes:_____

_____

_____

_____

_____

_____

_____

CHAPTER 24 - TITLE (OPTIONAL): _____

Notes:_____

_____

_____

_____

_____

_____

CHAPTER OUTLINE NOTES

CHAPTER 25 - TITLE (OPTIONAL): _____

Notes:_____

_____

_____

_____

_____

_____

_____

CHAPTER 26 - TITLE (OPTIONAL): _____

Notes:_____

_____

_____

_____

_____

_____

_____

CHAPTER 27 - TITLE (OPTIONAL): _____

Notes:_____

_____

_____

_____

_____

_____

CHAPTER OUTLINE NOTES

CHAPTER 28 - TITLE (OPTIONAL): _____

Notes:_____

_____

_____

_____

_____

_____

_____

_____

CHAPTER 29 - TITLE (OPTIONAL): _____

Notes:_____

_____

_____

_____

_____

_____

_____

_____

CHAPTER 30 - TITLE (OPTIONAL): _____

Notes:_____

_____

_____

_____

_____

_____

Section 3:
HONING YOUR CRAFT

POINT OF VIEW

If you've ever played a video game, you know the difference between first and third person. In writing, we call this the **POV (point of view)** or the **perspective**. Now, we'll show you how perspective can impact your writing.

First Person—I, me, we, mine.

Just like in a video game, first person shows the reader your world *directly* through the eyes of the main character. If the character doesn't see it, the reader doesn't see it. This perspective creates a closer emotional connection between the reader and the character. While internal dialogue is used in both options, it's most important in first person.

Example:

I always hated Mr. Kenny's house. It was ancient and smelled like dirty shoelaces. The draft from the paint-peeling windows made it colder inside than outside. But Mr. Kenny loved his old house and seeing him happy was all I cared about.

Strengths: Emotional depth, connection to the character.

Limitations: We only know what the character knows. Multiple POV's can be confusing for the reader.

Best for: Single POV, if using multiple POV's then make sure they have very distinct voices.

Books that used first person perspective:
- *Percy Jackson and the Olympians* by Rick Riordan
- *The Hunger Games* by Suzanne Collins
- *Diary of a Wimpy Kid* by Jeff Kinney

WHAT'S THE DIFFERENCE?

- **POV** is the method for narration: first person, second person, or third person.
- **Perspective** is how the character sees their world.

POINT OF VIEW & PERSPECTIVE

Third Person—He, she, they, their

Like in an open world adventure, third person gives the reader a wider view of your characters and world. Unlike first person, the narrator can reveal details that the character may not know, creating a sense of dread or anticipation. While internal dialogue is still important the reader's lens is a little further out, which can create dramatic and shocking revelations.

Example:

Gracie hated Mr. Kenny's house. It was ancient and smelled like dirty shoelaces. The draft from the paint-peeling windows made it colder inside than outside. But Mr. Kenny loved his old house. He was happy and that was all Gracie cared about.

Third person can be **limited** (the reader only knows what one character at a time knows) or **omniscient** (narrator knows and sees everything).

> **Strengths**: Wider world-building, multiple POVs.
>
> **Limitations**: Pulled back from character, less emotional connection.
>
> **Best for**: Complex plots, multiple POV's, good in every genre.

Books that used third person perspective:
- *A Wrinkle in Time* by Madeleine L'Engle
- *The Wild Robot* by Peter Brown
- *The Giver* by Lois Lowry

2nd Person—You, your

Second person puts the reader in the story. They are the main character. This can be great for role-playing games, choose your own adventure books, or other interactive fiction. Second person is not used as often as first or third person in novels. Not all readers enjoy being a part of the story, so we will not be going into detail about this perspective.

POINT OF VIEW & PERSPECTIVE

Sometime we can't decide what POV to write our book in!

One way to help is to write a scene in two ways. First write it as **first person**, then rewrite it as **third person**.

Write a scene in first person.

_____

_____

_____

_____

_____

_____

Write the same scene in third person.

_____

_____

_____

_____

_____

_____

_____

WRITING TERMS TO REMEMBER

Narrative - a story.
Narration - act of telling a story.
Narrator - a storyteller.

ACTIVE VS. PASSIVE VOICE

Before we explain the difference between active and passive voice, let's go over what **Voice** is.

Voice can be funneled into three primary types:

Narrative Voice:
Narrative voice can be defined by what technical choices you have made for your story, including POV, active or passive verbiage, sentence structure, and literary style. **Active** and **Passive** voice fall under the umbrella of narrative voice.

Character Voice:
Character voice, as you'd expect, is the unique way your character speaks and interacts with the world. It's important to try and give each and every one of your characters their own special flare! The goal is for readers to be able to tell who's speaking even without dialogue tags.

Authorial Voice:
Authorial voice is your one-of-a-kind **style of writing**! Maybe you like quick, snappy sentences. Maybe you often use long, flowery descriptions. Whatever the case may be, eventually, as you continue to practice your craft, your authorial voice will form on its own. Don't stress about trying to force this skill to develop before its time!

Now let's dive into active and passive voice.

While both styles have their place, it's **important to use the active voice as much as possible**. Why? Because it creates a sense of **immediacy and immersion** into your character's POV that **passive** voice can't capture.

In the **active** voice, the subject of the sentence is the performer of the action. In the **passive**, the performer of the sentence is receiving the action. An easy way to tell if your sentence is active or passive is to find where your character's name lands within it.

Is their name *before* the action? Probably **active**.
Does their name come *after* the action? Probably **passive**.

ACTIVE VS. PASSIVE VOICE

Sometimes it's hard to tell the difference!

Another quick way to tell is if you have the words **"was"** or **"by"** in your sentence. This **often points** to the **passive** voice.

Even for experienced writers, learning the difference—and properly using—the two styles can be difficult. Instead of just trying to tell the difference, we're going to show you.

ACTIVE

"Dean chased down the androids."

See how Dean is the performer of the sentence? Also, his name comes before the androids, who are the receivers of the action.

PASSIVE

"The androids were chased by Dean."

In this sentence, the receiver (the androids) come before both the action and the performer, creating a less exciting and dramatic tone. See also how the word "by" ended up in there? A solid clue to sniff out a passive sentence.

DIALOGUE: WHO IS TALKING?

Dialogue is how characters talk, who is talking, and how we write it on the page. In this section, we talk about how to learn and practice the craft of dialogue!

Dialogue Tags

In a story, the writer will use quotation marks to tell the reader when a character is speaking. They will also use something called *dialogue tags*. These "tags" can follow the character's speech, be placed in the middle, or come after it. The purpose of dialogue tags and quotation marks is to prevent confusion about who is talking or what is happening in the story.

Here are some examples:

Fred walked into the room and yelled, "No! Don't touch that, it's hot!"

> **Before** the dialogue tag, we see Fred before we hear what he said.

"No," Emily said. "It's cold now. No need to worry."

> **In the middle** of the dialogue tag, we indicate that Emily is speaking.

"That is a relief." Fred wiped a hand down his face.

> **After** of the dialogue tag, we know Fred is relieved by his actions.

A dialogue tag can be how someone said something (**descriptive**), the way they said it (**tonal**), or what they are doing as they speak (**action**).

 NOW YOU TRY!

On the next pages we will practice using dialogue tags to make our characters' conversations both readable and interesting.

DIALOGUE TAGS: DESCRIPTIVE

Descriptive (How They Said It)

Practice using descriptive dialogue tags. *Make three sentences using the provided tags or make up your own.* See example below.

"I plan to join the race," she said.

"What will you do if you lose?" he asked.

DESCRIPTIVE TAGS

- Said
- Asked
- Chuckled
- Smiled

- Argued
- Grinned
- Laughed
- Shouted

- Yelled
- Exclaimed
- Announced
- Whispered

Sentence 1

_____

_____

Sentence 2

_____

_____

Sentence 3

_____

_____

DIALOGUE TAGS: TONAL

Tonal (The Way They Said It)

Tone can be made in a couple of different ways with dialogue. Sometimes a writer will use both *what* the character is saying and the *way* they say it to show tone. Here is an example:

> *"You're right," she huffed. "I love cleaning my room."*
>
> *"If you are so good at it, why don't you give it a try?" he teased.*

The way a character says something can really change the meaning of what they are saying. Using punctuation can also help with creating tone.

> *"I have never traveled by sea," he sighed, "and I never will . . ."*
>
> *"I have never traveled by sea," he muttered, "and I never will!"*

Make three sentences using the provided tonal dialogue tags or make up your own.

TONAL TAGS

- Growled
- Roared
- Huffed
- Cried

- Scolded
- Muttered
- Murmured
- Sighed

- Gasped
- Purred
- Scoffed
- Jeered

- Grumbled
- Pleaded
- Boasted
- Snarled

Sentence 1

_____

Sentence 2

_____

Sentence 3

_____

DIALOGUE TAGS: ACTION

Action (What They Are Doing as They Speak)
Using too many different descriptive or tone tags can be a distraction. Sometimes "said" is just as good in most situations. However, if you are tired of using "said" all the time, you can use action as an alternative! Actions can also help your reader understand who is talking and what their tone is.

"I didn't want this!" Caleb threw his cereal on the floor.

Mom bent over to pick up the bowl and asked, "Is that how we treat our food?"

"That is unacceptable." Dad glared at Caleb. "What do you say to your mother?"

"I'm sorry," Caleb slumped into his seat.

Now is your chance to practice using action tags to break up your dialogue. ***Make three sentences using only action tags before, after, or in-between speech.***

Sentence 1

_____

_____

Sentence 2

_____

_____

Sentence 3

_____

_____

DIALOGUE PACING

Pacing Dialogue

Not every line of dialogue needs a dialogue tag. You can balance how many tags you are using and what you are using by remembering what dialogue tags are for. We use tags to help our reader learn something about the situation or the character or to let them know who is speaking. If the dialogue is going back and forth between two characters, maybe you don't need a dialogue tag at all. Using limited tags can help with pacing your story.

Here is an example of limited dialogue tags:

"What time is the movie?" Harry asked.

"I don't know. I thought you were getting the tickets." Julie stared at him.

"Oh no."

"Oh no, what? You did get the tickets, right?"

"Well, here is the thing..." Harry bit his lip. "I may—"

"You forgot, didn't you?"

"Yeah."

 **NOW YOU TRY!**

On the next page write a short scene between two characters. Let us know who is speaking at the beginning, and then try to write their conversation with limited dialogue tags. Use a mix of descriptive, tonal, and action tags. Try to occasionally use no tag at all if you don't think you need it.

Here is an idea if you need one: Two friends find out they are trying out for the same part in the school play.

DIALOGUE PACING

Write a scene with dialogue between two characters.

_____

_____

_____

_____

_____

_____

_____

_____

_____

_____

_____

_____

_____

_____

_____

_____

_____

_____

_____

DIALOGUE TAGS: CONTEXT

Dialogue Tags Can Change the Meaning

Dialogue tags can help us reveal things about our characters in a short amount of time. They can help us increase the tension of the scene. The tag "snarled" feels angry or protective, whereas "whispered" may make the speech sound secretive.

"I can't finish my homework," she muttered.

"I can't finish my homework!" she shouted.

"I can't finish my homework," she cried.

Now you give it a try. **Choose your own tag to finish the sentence. Try to pick tags that change the meaning of what the character is saying.**

*"I can't believe you," he*_____.

*"I can't believe you," he*_____.

*"I can't believe you," he*_____.

Dialogue can make or break a story. It can also be one of the trickiest skills in writing to master. While dialogue should feel natural and real, it shouldn't always include the slang or repetitive phrases we often use with friends.

1. Decide the Era and Setting

First, decide when and where your story takes place. Is it modern-day? The eighties? A fantasy world set in medieval times? Knowing this will help keep your dialogue culturally accurate and consistent with the world your characters inhabit.

2. Keep It Natural

Remember, your characters are people! Do you use your friend's name every other word in a sentence? Probably not. Avoid unnecessary repetition or overloading dialogue with information the characters already know.

DIALOGUE: WHO IS TALKING?

Here's an example of what NOT to do:

"Hey, Nancy, it's so great that you agreed to babysit my sister, Tabby. If you hadn't, I wouldn't be able to go to my brother, Dylan's, soccer practice. If you don't remember, soccer is very important to him. You're the best, Nancy! Did I mention your name is Nancy?"

See how awkward that sounds? Keep it natural! Instead of cramming everything into one line, let the story reveal details through actions or narration.

3. Avoid the Maid and Butler Scenario
This happens when characters use dialogue to explain things they already know, just to give the reader context.

Instead of saying:

"Nancy, thanks for babysitting Tabby so I can go to Dylan's soccer practice. Soccer is really important to him."

Try this:

Nancy picked up Tabby's favorite book. "I've got this covered. Go cheer for Dylan!"
"Thanks, Nancy." I grabbed my keys. "Soccer's his whole life."

This version feels more natural and allows the reader to piece together the situation without being told outright.

Tip!

Read your dialogue out loud! If it doesn't sound like something a real person would say, tweak it until it feels right.

CHEAT SHEET: DIALOGUE

DESCRIPTIVE TAGS

- Said
- Asked
- Chuckled
- Smiled

- Argued
- Grinned
- Laughed
- Shouted

- Yelled
- Exclaimed
- Announced
- Whispered

TONAL TAGS

- Growled
- Roared
- Huffed
- Cried

- Scolded
- Muttered
- Murmured
- Sighed

- Gasped
- Purred
- Scoffed
- Jeered

- Grumbled
- Pleaded
- Boasted
- Snarled

Avoid Overusing Dialogue Tags

Reminder that using "asked" or "said" is perfectly fine! Using too many different dialogue tags can be distracting for the reader. Sometimes the words a character is saying or how you punctuated it is enough to get your idea across.

Overusing tags examples:

- *"This is the worst day ever!" she stomped angrily.*
- *"You know nothing about my job!" he shouted defensively.*
- *"I thought you already knew," she teased gleefully.*

Better alternative:

- *"This is the worst day ever!" she said.*
- *"You know nothing about my job!" he said.*
- *"I thought you already knew." She crossed her arms.*

CHEAT SHEET: DIALOGUE

Tip! Actions tags are a great replacement for overused dialogue tags

Watch out for common mistakes!

Using the wrong punctuation

Knowing where to put your comma or periods in dialogue can be tricky! It can also be tricky to figure out when you capitalize a word and when you don't.

Rules to remember:

- Punctuation goes inside the quotations.
- If a tag follows the dialogue use a comma.
- If action follows the dialogue use a period.
- Capitalize names always.

Incorrect

- *"What is behind that door"? She asked.*
- *"I will train the magician." He said.*
- *"Wait! I will take it outside," she tucked the rabbit into her coat and left.*

Correct

Put punctuation inside:
- *"What is behind that door?" she asked.*

Use comma for dialogue tag
- *"I will train the magician," he said with a laugh.*

Use period for action tag:
- *"Wait! I will take it outside." She tucked the rabbit into her coat and left.*

IMAGERY & DESCRIPTION

You may have heard the old adage "Show, don't Tell."

Good. Remember it. Engrain it into your DNA. The greatest tool you have available to lock in a reader is creating something they can feel with **all 5 senses**. This may sound silly, but we promise, it's an essential skill to master.

If your character walks into a musty hotel room, you can set the scene for the reader by showing them, instead of telling them what your character is experiencing. **Let us give you an example:**

Telling:
Jane stepped into her hotel room. The room was old and dirty, and the bedsheets were crumpled on the floor.

Showing:
As Jane twisted the brass doorknob on hotel room 101, the door creaked open, as if on its own. She crinkled her nose as the stench of mildew forced its way up her nostrils. Great. Jane yelped when her foot slid on the pile of bedsheets curled up on the dingy floorboards. Pain twanged through her ankle. This vacation was starting swimmingly.

NOW YOU TRY!

On the next page use the prompt to show instead of tell the scene. Use all five sense and give it personality.

IMAGERY & DESCRIPTION

Prompt: *A deer interrupts Thanksgiving dinner by sneaking into the kitchen and eating the food.*

What would this scene *smell* like?

_____

_____

What would this scene *taste* like?

_____

_____

What would this scene *feel* like?

_____

_____

What would this scene *look* like?

_____

_____

What would this scene *sound* like?

_____

_____

Now write it all together.

_____

_____

_____

_____

_____

MAKE IT TENSE

Tension in a story is the way that you create a sense of impending doom or anticipation for the reader. It's also the number one way to keep your reader **hooked** and continuing to turn the pages.

There are bazillions of ways to create tension, but they all boil down to one concept—**delaying the release of information.**

Why do you read a mystery? To see how it's solved, of course! But would you keep reading if the mystery was solved in the first chapter? Probably not. Spoon feeding readers only the information they need WHEN they need it keeps your tension high. Don't lay out all your cards at once.

MAKE IT TENSE!

Prompt: Your character is trying to sleep but something is growling under the bed. Build tension by **delaying the release of information**.

_____

_____

_____

_____

_____

The easiest way to **add tension to any story is to give your character a deep, dark secret.** Another way is to **give them an internal flaw that directly conflicts with their role** in the story.

Example: A kid with social anxiety is required to make a public speech. Not only will the readers be DYING to know what happens next, they'll also be rooting for your character to grow and succeed!

I must know what happens!

Section 4:
RESOURCES & GUIDES

WHERE DO IDEAS COME FROM?

The number one question we get as a writers is "Where do your ideas come from?" The answer is simple. Ideas come from anywhere and everywhere! We can be inspired by almost anything and so can you!

You can find inspiration for stories everywhere; you just have to look! While you can always do a quick internet search for writing prompts, you can just step outside to find materials to work with.

Here is a quick list of great sources for ideas.

 People watch. Think about the people you see at the grocery store. What are their lives like? Maybe the cart pusher is actually a government spy on a mission to stop a terrorist.

 Explore Nature. What about that giant storm cloud rolling in? What if it sucked people into it like a vacuum and your character has to figure out how to rescue them?

 **Study the world and have fun.** This may sound weird, but ideas are cheap. Don't get yourself stuck by trying to force ONE idea to work. Enjoy yourself! Take something you observe and twist it into something fun and new!

WHERE DO IDEAS COME FROM?

Still need inspiration? Since we're so generous, here are a few prompts for you to try:

- You live in a city that floods twice a day.

- You're babysitting a super genius toddler that keeps escaping.

- Spiders mobilize to take over Earth.

- You have two months to become an Olympic track star. Problem is, you're a mermaid.

- Airplane crash survivors find themselves on an island overrun with giants.

- You just found out you've inherited one billion dollars from a relative you didn't know about.

- At night, you transform into a different person.

- There are two warring tribes, and your best friend is from the other.

- You learn that you were kidnapped as a baby and are actually the long-lost prince/princess of a wealthy kingdom.

- You can talk to animals and volunteer at an animal shelter.

- You can see into other people's futures, but never your own.

- Your best friend goes missing and no one seems to have noticed. You have to solve the mystery of her disappearance alone.

- You not only are a rockstar, but you're also a superhero that has to keep their identity hidden from their fans.

- You find a magic sketch book that makes everything you draw come to life.

- You work at a shelter for injured dragons that can no longer fly.

WRITER'S BLOCK

Oh, the dreaded writer's block! The moment where your mind goes blank and you don't know where to take your story next. Every writer has their own method for overcoming it. Here are some ideas you can try when you are stuck. Hopefully, one of these ideas will get your creativity flowing.

CREATIVE TECHNIQUES

- **Freewriting** – Set a timer and write without worrying about grammar or structure. Sometimes freeing your mind will spark new and interesting ideas!
- **Writing prompts** - pick a writing prompt from online or in this book and try
- it out.
- **Brainstorming** – Write a list of ideas, questions, or problems. No idea is a bad idea. Just some ideas are better. Make a big list!
- **Skip the scene** – Write a note like "and a soccer game happens here" and move on.
- **Review your notes** – Consider what might be the cause. If you are unclear about your story this can often cause writer's block. Take a moment to reflect on what may be stopping your writing flow. If you can identify and address the root cause, you'll be back to writing in no time.
- **Join a writer's group** – Being part of a larger group of writers can be inspiring. Writer's groups support each other in overcoming blocks, generating solutions, and listening to each other's woes. You are not alone!

ENVIRONMENTAL CHANGES

- **Set the mood** – Create a habit such as a cup you always use, or a chair you like to sit in and set up your environment for writing.
- **Listen to music** – Find songs that match the vibes of your story. Close your eyes and imagine scenes playing out like a movie.
- **Move around** – Take a walk outside, visit a coffee shop, or head to the library.
- **Take a break** – Work on a different project, do a hobby, or even take a nap.

WRITER'S BLOCK

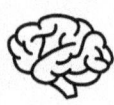 **MENTAL RESTS**

- **Consume media** – Watch a TV show, enjoy a movie, or read a book.
- **Ask a friend** – Talk with someone about your story. Ask them questions to get their perspective.

Remember all progress is still progress. Writer's block can slow us down but even if you write one page or a hundred words, you're still working towards your goal!

Pick one idea and see if it will ignite your story again.

WHAT IS A GENRE?

Genres

There are a MILLION genres and subgenres. It can be extremely overwhelming to figure out where your story falls on the genre ladder! It's important to remember that genres can be mixed and matched with each other. You don't have to only pick one! Explore. Have fun with it. To get you started off, here's a list of some basic and recognizable fiction genres.

Subgenres

A subgenre is a smaller category in the bigger category. Example would be historical romance or sci-fi detective stories. When we blend or bend genres by mixing them, we can really see some interesting stories!

FANTASY: Dragons! Magic! Incredible, zany worlds that are beyond imagination! You don't have to go to that extreme. One way to define fantasy is that its contents will never be reality.

SCIENCE FICTION: Robots! Spaceships! Sweet, cyber gadgets galore! There are many different forms of sci-fi (military, space-opera, etc) but another definition is that sci-fi content could be, maybe in the far, far future.

HORROR: This genre is meant to scare the reader. Whether it be with physical horror, monster horror, psychological horror—you want your readers to be hiding under their puffy, pink blankets.

THRILLER: If you've ever watched a movie with gunfights, car chases, and secret agents, you were probably watching a thriller. The heart of a thriller is the tension. Hearts need to be pounding. You're on the edge of your seat. Of course, thrillers don't have to be in modern times. You could make a caveman thriller, if you really wanted. Just make sure it's tense!

CONTEMPORARY: Speaking of modern times, that's really all contemporary means. If your story has modern technology and inventions, it's probably one of the many forms of contemporary.

GENRES & SUBGENRES

 **ROMANCE**: We all know what romance is, but it's important to remember that romance comes in many colors and levels. It could be a sweet, small-town romance. A fantasy romance. Hey, maybe even a romance that forms while running from a chain-saw killer, the world is your oyster!

 **MYSTERY**: Ever read or watched Sherlock Holmes? Listened to a true crime podcast? Mystery is all about the who-dunnit. Whether it's solving a crime, a centuries old fable, a treasure hunt, cozy secrets, courtroom stories—there are many options to explore.

Writing can be categorized in countless ways. We only covered some of the popular fiction genres but there are so many more literary genres out there. Think about biographies, self-help books, textbooks, poetry, nonfiction, history books--the options are endless.

What is your book's genre? (Does is have a subgenre?)

_____

_____

What are two genres you'd like to see mixed together?

_____

_____

AFTER DRAFT 1: REVISING

Congrats! You have finished your first draft of your novel.

Even if you think it's perfect, every first draft needs a stern eye to discover things we didn't see in our first round. So, what are the next steps? There are three major steps after you finish your first draft: revising, editing, and proofreading.

Revising

Revising is the next step after your first draft. This is the start of draft two! The focus of revising is "big picture" problems. These are big changes like fixing plot holes, a missing character, or adding a needed scene. Maybe you forgot there was a dog on the spaceship, and you must choose to either write him back in or write him out completely (we vote to keep the dog). This is the time to ask questions about your story and evaluate the structure you created. Revising is about making your story flow.

REVISING CHECKLIST:

- ☐ Did the problem get solved? (*What is Your Problem?, pg 7*)
- ☐ Did the protagonist get what they needed in the end? (*Building Character: Wants vs Needs, pg 9*)
- ☐ Did the main characters' arcs feel complete or resolved? (*What is an Arc?, pg 30*)
- ☐ Are there places where we can add more tension? (*Make It Tense, pg 75*)
- ☐ Is this scene necessary? Do I need another scene?
- ☐ Can I tighten my dialogue? (*Dialogue, pg 63-72*)
- ☐ Have I repeated anything too much?
- ☐ Are there places where things are confusing?
- ☐ Are there places where I tell more than I show? (*Imagery & Description, pg 73-74*)
- ☐ Are there places where we need more description?
- ☐ Is each setting/location following the rules I set? (*Setting, pg 23-27*)
- ☐ Is my theme evident without being a lecture? (*Discovery Your Theme, pg 28*)
- ☐ Did I tie up all the loose ends?
- ☐ Are character/setting descriptions consistent?

AFTER DRAFT 2: EDITING AND PROOFING

Editing

After we have revised our draft to our heart's desire, it's time to really start editing. Editing is focused on sentence structure, grammar, and spelling. It's about taking the story we have refined and improving the readability and conciseness. Perhaps you have already done some editing in the revising stage as they can overlap. Editing is when we really dig as deep as we can to make things correct.

EDITING CHECKLIST:

- ☐ Did I spell each character's name correctly and the same way every time?
- ☐ Did I spell the places correctly and the same way every time?
- ☐ Did I check for capitalization?
- ☐ Did I vary my sentences to make them interesting?
- ☐ When I read the dialogue, can I tell who is speaking?
- ☐ Did I fix any grammar or spelling mistakes? (Use cheat sheets if needed.)

Proofreading

You've filled in all the plot holes and caught all your grammar bugs. The next step is to proofread. Proofreading is the art of double-checking. Pull out your notes from revising and editing and ensure they are all completed and marked off. We all make mistakes, and after looking over our work for hours, it's easy to miss things.

Proofreading Tips:
- **Read out loud:** When we read out loud, we can catch spelling, grammar, and awkward sentences more easily.
- **Change the font:** Some writers trick their brains into seeing their manuscript differently by changing the font. It makes it feel like a whole new story.
- **Print it out:** Double-space and print your manuscript. Just like your teacher, take a pen and write between the lines the changes you want.
- **Turn on Text-to-Speech:** Most word processing programs can read your writing back to you. This is a great way to catch problems, especially if you are an audio learner.
- **Get an extra set of eyes:** It helps to have another writer look over your work. They usually can catch things we didn't see in our drafting process.

PUNCTUATION CHEAT SHEET

There are so many rules and things to look out for in punctuation. Here is a quick cheat sheet for some of the most common rules.

 ## COMMA RULES

Sometimes it can feel that comma rules are always changing! But there are many rules that commas do follow. Here are some major ones to look out for.

You Need a Comma:

- **After a coordinating conjunction:** - What is a coordinating conjunction? All you need to remember is FANBOYS (for, and, nor, but, or, yet, so).

    I wanted to stay home, but I had to go to work.

- **After an adverb clause that begins a sentence:** - Adverb clauses usually start with words like: after, although, as, because, when, where, etc.

    When I am done eating, I plan to wash my plate.

- **After an introductory phrase or word-** Introductory phrases or words set the stage for the main part of the sentence.

    In the morning, we can ride our bikes.

- **To separate a list or series of three or more items -** Note: The comma before "and" is optional—just pick one style and stay consistent!

    Before we leave, make sure you have your shoes, keys, wallet and cellphone.
Also acceptable: *Before we leave, make sure you have your shoes, keys, wallet, and cellphone.*

- **To separate extra information:**

    My friend, the barber, will cut my hair this week.

- **With dialogue tags -** See Who is Talking? (*pg 70*) for more examples.

    "You won't believe what I saw today," he said, "there was an elephant in the garden."
    "I forgot about it," she said. "Tomorrow, I will set an alarm."
    I told them, "Knock it off! You'll wake the baby!"

PUNCTUATION CHEAT SHEET

You Don't Need a Comma:

- **When punctuation replaces it:**

  *"Wait!" she said. **(The exclamation point replaces the comma.)***
  *"What do you mean?" he asked. **(The question mark replaces the comma.)***

- **Between the subject and the verb:**

  ☑ Incorrect: Whoever turned on the oven, forgot to turn it off.

  ⊗ Correct: Whoever turned on the oven forgot to turn it off.

 # APOSTROPHE RULES

When to Use an Apostrophe:

To tell us the word is plural for letters or symbols - Apostrophes are used to make letters or symbols plural, but not for regular nouns.

- *My report card said I have all C's.*
- *I shouldn't have said so many um's in my speech.*

For contractions - Contractions use apostrophes to show missing letters.

- didn't = did not
- shouldn't = should not
- it's = it is
- hasn't = has not

To show possession - Apostrophes are used to show when something belongs to someone or something.

- *My brother's truck is parked there.* (One brother owns the truck.)
- *My brothers love trucks.* (No apostrophe—just plural.)
- *My brothers' truck is parked there.* (The truck belongs to multiple brothers.)
- Important Note: *Its* and *it's* can be confusing!
  - It's = It is (It's time to go.)
  - Its = Possessive form of "it" (The truck starts its engine.)

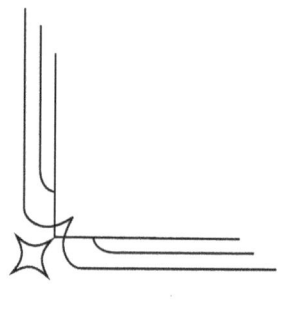

PUNCTUATION CHEAT SHEET

Plural Nouns and Apostrophes:

Plural nouns can make apostrophes complicated, especially when nouns end in y or s. Here's how to handle them:

Nouns Ending in Y

- Baby = Singular noun
- Baby's = Singular possessive (e.g., The baby's toy is on the floor.)
- Babies = Plural noun
- Babies' = Plural possessive (e.g., The babies' toys are on the floor.)

Nouns Ending in S

- Dress = Singular noun
- Dress's = Singular possessive (e.g., The dress's color is beautiful.)
- Dresses = Plural noun
- Dresses' = Plural possessive (e.g., The dresses' colors are beautiful.)

 # ITALICIZING RULES

Italics can be used in storytelling to enhance the reader's experience. Writers use italics in specific ways:

Create Emphasis:
- Italics can be used to emphasize a particular word or phrase.
  - ***Example:*** He didn't mind having a lab partner, but out of all his classmates, the teacher assigned *her*.

Internal Dialogue:
- Italics are often used to show that a character is thinking rather than speaking out loud.
  - ***Example:*** *Wait! Did I just say that out loud?*

Certain Scenes:
- Italics can be used to distinguish unique elements, such as dream sequences, flashbacks, or time jumps. This helps the reader identify that something is different about the text.

Titles for Larger Works of Art:
- Italicize movie titles, book titles, and titles of other larger works of art. For smaller things like poems, TV episodes, etc.--put them in quotations.

PUNCTUATION CHEAT SHEET

 ## DASH RULES

There are two common types of dashes:
- En Dash (–): Shorter and often used like a hyphen.
- Em Dash (—): Longer and used in more dynamic ways in writing.

1. Em Dash (—)
The em dash is versatile and can replace other punctuation marks like commas or colons in some cases.

> **Interrupting a Thought or Conversation:**
> *Example:*
>
> *"I asked about it last night—wait, you weren't there last night!"*
>
> *"Did you see where the tiger went—" Isaac began to ask.*
>
> *"I see him, right there!" Joe cut him off.*
>
> **Making a Colon Less Formal:**
> *Example:*
>
> *We always order the best cereal—Captain Krisps, CocoPops, and Fruity Crunches.*
>
> **Replacing Commas in Lists for Clarity:**
> - Em dashes can make sentences with many commas more formal or easier to read.
>   - ***Comma Example:*** *The boys, Peter, Jarod, and Michael, formed the chess club.*
>   - ***Em Dash Example:*** *The boys—Peter, Jarod, and Michael—formed the chess club.*

2. En Dash/Hyphen (–)
The en dash (or hyphen) is shorter and used in specific scenarios:

> **Joining Two or More Words That Describe a Noun:**
> - *She leaped into the green-murky water.*
>
> **Compound Words:**
> - *Brother-in-law*
>
> **Connecting Phrases Before Nouns:**
> - *12-year-old boy*
>
> **Numbers Ranging from 21–99:**
> - *Twenty-three, fifty-two*
>
> **When a Prefix and Root Word Share the Same Vowel:**
> - *Re-engagement*

These are just some of the rules for punctuation. If you come across a confusing situation and aren't sure how to handle it, a quick online search can usually provide the answer. Don't hesitate to double-check—everyone needs a little help now and then!

CAPITALIZATION CHEAT SHEET

 ## CAPITALIZATION RULES

When to Capitalize:

The Pronoun "I" - Always capitalize the pronoun "I."

- *I am ready!*

Proper Nouns - Proper nouns include the names of people, places, and specifically mentioned things.

Examples:

- **People:** Jerry, Bob, Barbara, Timory, Jenna, Astrid, Spock
- **Places:** Mt. Rainier, England, Washington State, Africa, Pacific Northwest, China
- **Things:** The Constitution, English, Calculus 1

Titles - Capitalizing titles follows specific rules:

Rule 1: Capitalize the first and last word.

- *A Christmas Carol*
- *Star Wars*

Rule 2: Capitalize all major words, including verbs, adverbs, and adjectives.

- *Alice in Wonderland*
- *A Series of Unfortunate Events*
- *The Very Hungry Caterpillar*

Rule 3: Don't capitalize minor words like and, the, in, etc., unless they are the first or last word.

- *The Cat in the Hat*
- *If You Give a Mouse a Cookie*
- *Percy Jackson and the Olympians: The Lightning Thief*

Rule 4: Capitalize prepositions when they function as adverbs.

- *Look Up the Road* (Up functions as an adverb here.)

CAPITALIZATION CHEAT SHEET

Trademarks: Always capitalize trademarked names.

- Ex: Kleenex and Band-Aid
- If you don't want to use trademarked names, use generic alternatives like tissue or bandage.

Company Names: Always capitalize company names.

- Ex: Walmart, Costco, Microsoft
- Even fictional company names should be capitalized. For example, if your character is shopping at BuyMart (a fictional store), it should be capitalized.

Honorifics

An honorific is a title or term of respect for a person's position or role.

- **Capitalize honorifics when used with a name:**
  - Ex: Mr., Mrs., Dr., Lord, King, Queen, Capt., Lt.
- **Capitalize honorifics used as a substitute for a name:**
  - Ex: Your Highness, Your Majesty, Your Holiness, Father

it's a lot to remember!

Section 5:
ADDITIONAL WORKSHEETS

BUILDING CHARACTER: WANTS VS. NEEDS

Character's name: _____

Who are they in the story? (circle one)

Protagonist   Antagonist   Side Character   Other: _____

What does this character want?

_____

_____

_____

What does this character *actually* need?

_____

_____

_____

_____

How will you connect what they want with what they need?

_____

_____

_____

_____

BUILDING CHARACTER: WANTS VS. NEEDS

Character's name: _____

Who are they in the story? (circle one)

     Protagonist   Antagonist   Side Character   Other: _____

What does this character want?

_____

_____

_____

What does this character *actually* need?

_____

_____

_____

_____

How will you connect what they want with what they need?

_____

_____

_____

_____

BUILDING CHARACTER: WANTS VS. NEEDS

Character's name: _____

Who are they in the story? (circle one)

      Protagonist   Antagonist   Side Character   Other: _____

What does this character want?

_____

_____

_____

What does this character *actually* need?

_____

_____

_____

_____

How will you connect what they want with what they need?

_____

_____

_____

_____

BUILDING CHARACTER: WANTS VS. NEEDS

Character's name: _____

Who are they in the story? (circle one)

Protagonist   Antagonist   Side Character   Other: _____

What does this character want?

_____

_____

_____

What does this character *actually* need?

_____

_____

_____

_____

How will you connect what they want with what they need?

_____

_____

_____

_____

CHARACTER SHEET

Draw or tape character
inspiration here.

First Name:_____

Last Name: _____

Physical Description: _____

_____

_____

_____

Age: _____

What does this character *want*? _____

What does this character *need*?_____

What are their flaws?_____
(*Check Flaws page 21 for ideas, pick no more than 2*)

What are their quirks?_____
(*Check Quirks Page 20 for ideas, pick no more than 2*)

Where do they live?_____

What do they do?_____

What do they love? _____

List things they hate: _____

List things they are good at: _____

List things they are bad at: _____

CHARACTER SHEET

What is their family like? _____

_____

_____

_____

_____

_____

_____

_____

What is their backstory? _____

_____

_____

_____

_____

_____

_____

_____

_____

_____

CHARACTER SHEET

Draw or tape character
inspiration here.

First Name:_____

Last Name: _____

Physical Description: _____

_____

_____

_____

Age: _____

What does this character *want*? _____

What does this character *need*?_____

What are their flaws?_____
(*Check Flaws page 21 for ideas, pick no more than 2*)

What are their quirks?_____
(*Check Quirks Page 20 for ideas, pick no more than 2*)

Where do they live?_____

What do they do?_____

What do they love? _____

List things they hate: _____

List things they are good at: _____

List things they are bad at: _____

CHARACTER SHEET

What is their family like? _____

_____

_____

_____

_____

_____

_____

_____

_____

What is their backstory? _____

_____

_____

_____

_____

_____

_____

_____

_____

_____

_____

CHARACTER SHEET

Draw or tape character
inspiration here.

First Name:_____

Last Name: _____

Physical Description: _____

_____

_____

_____

Age: _____

What does this character *want*? _____

What does this character *need*?_____

What are their flaws?_____
(*Check Flaws page 21 for ideas, pick no more than 2*)

What are their quirks?_____
(*Check Quirks Page 20 for ideas, pick no more than 2*)

Where do they live?_____

What do they do?_____

What do they love? _____

List things they hate: _____

List things they are good at: _____

List things they are bad at: _____

CHARACTER SHEET

What is their family like? _____

_____

_____

_____

_____

_____

_____

_____

What is their backstory? _____

_____

_____

_____

_____

_____

_____

_____

_____

_____

_____

CHARACTER SHEET

Draw or tape character
inspiration here.

First Name:_____

Last Name: _____

Physical Description: _____

_____

_____

_____

Age: _____

What does this character *want*? _____

What does this character *need*?_____

What are their flaws?_____
(*Check Flaws page 21 for ideas, pick no more than 2*)

What are their quirks?_____
(*Check Quirks Page 20 for ideas, pick no more than 2*)

Where do they live?_____

What do they do?_____

What do they love? _____

List things they hate: _____

List things they are good at: _____

List things they are bad at: _____

CHARACTER SHEET

What is their family like? _____

_____

_____

_____

_____

_____

_____

_____

What is their backstory? _____

_____

_____

_____

_____

_____

_____

_____

_____

_____

_____

CHARACTER SHEET

Draw or tape character inspiration here.

First Name:_____

Last Name: _____

Physical Description: _____

_____

_____

_____

Age: _____

What does this character *want*? _____

What does this character *need*?_____

What are their flaws?_____
(*Check Flaws page 21 for ideas, pick no more than 2*)

What are their quirks?_____
(*Check Quirks Page 20 for ideas, pick no more than 2*)

Where do they live?_____

What do they do?_____

What do they love? _____

List things they hate: _____

List things they are good at: _____

List things they are bad at: _____

CHARACTER SHEET

What is their family like? _____

_____

_____

_____

_____

_____

_____

_____

What is their backstory? _____

_____

_____

_____

_____

_____

_____

_____

_____

_____

_____

_____

CHARACTER SHEET

Draw or tape character inspiration here.

First Name:_____

Last Name: _____

Physical Description: _____

_____

_____

_____

Age: _____

What does this character *want*? _____

What does this character *need*?_____

What are their flaws?_____
(*Check Flaws page 21 for ideas, pick no more than 2*)

What are their quirks?_____
(*Check Quirks Page 20 for ideas, pick no more than 2*)

Where do they live?_____

What do they do?_____

What do they love? _____

List things they hate: _____

List things they are good at: _____

List things they are bad at: _____

CHARACTER SHEET

What is their family like? _____

_____

_____

_____

_____

_____

_____

_____

What is their backstory? _____

_____

_____

_____

_____

_____

_____

_____

_____

_____

_____

CHARACTER SHEET

Draw or tape character
inspiration here.

First Name:_____

Last Name: _____

Physical Description: _____

_____

_____

_____

Age: _____

What does this character *want*? _____

What does this character *need*? _____

What are their flaws? _____
(*Check Flaws page 21 for ideas, pick no more than 2*)

What are their quirks? _____
(*Check Quirks Page 20 for ideas, pick no more than 2*)

Where do they live? _____

What do they do? _____

What do they love? _____

List things they hate: _____

List things they are good at: _____

List things they are bad at: _____

CHARACTER SHEET

What is their family like? _____

_____

_____

_____

_____

_____

_____

_____

_____

_____

What is their backstory? _____

_____

_____

_____

_____

_____

_____

_____

_____

_____

_____

_____

_____

CHARACTER SHEET

Draw or tape character
inspiration here.

First Name:_____

Last Name: _____

Physical Description: _____

_____

_____

_____

Age: _____

What does this character *want*? _____

What does this character *need*?_____

What are their flaws?_____
(*Check Flaws page 21 for ideas, pick no more than 2*)

What are their quirks?_____
(*Check Quirks Page 20 for ideas, pick no more than 2*)

Where do they live?_____

What do they do?_____

What do they love? _____

List things they hate: _____

List things they are good at: _____

List things they are bad at: _____

CHARACTER SHEET

What is their family like? _____

_____

_____

_____

_____

_____

_____

_____

_____

_____

What is their backstory? _____

_____

_____

_____

_____

_____

_____

_____

_____

_____

_____

_____

_____

CHARACTER SHEET

[Draw or tape character inspiration here.]

First Name:_____

Last Name: _____

Physical Description: _____

_____

_____

_____

Age: _____

What does this character *want*? _____

What does this character *need*?_____

What are their flaws?_____
(*Check Flaws page 21 for ideas, pick no more than 2*)

What are their quirks?_____
(*Check Quirks Page 20 for ideas, pick no more than 2*)

Where do they live?_____

What do they do?_____

What do they love? _____

List things they hate: _____

List things they are good at: _____

List things they are bad at: _____

CHARACTER SHEET

What is their family like? _____

_____

_____

_____

_____

_____

_____

_____

_____

What is their backstory? _____

_____

_____

_____

_____

_____

_____

_____

_____

_____

_____

_____

CHARACTER SHEET

Draw or tape character
inspiration here.

First Name:_____

Last Name: _____

Physical Description: _____

_____

_____

_____

Age: _____

What does this character *want*? _____

What does this character *need*?_____

What are their flaws?_____
(*Check Flaws page 21 for ideas, pick no more than 2*)

What are their quirks?_____
(*Check Quirks Page 20 for ideas, pick no more than 2*)

Where do they live?_____

What do they do?_____

What do they love? _____

List things they hate: _____

List things they are good at: _____

List things they are bad at: _____

CHARACTER SHEET

What is their family like? _____

_____

_____

_____

_____

_____

_____

_____

_____

What is their backstory? _____

_____

_____

_____

_____

_____

_____

_____

_____

_____

_____

_____

CHARACTER SHEET

Draw or tape character
inspiration here.

First Name:_____

Last Name: _____

Physical Description: _____

_____

_____

_____

Age: _____

What does this character *want*? _____

What does this character *need*?_____

What are their flaws?_____
(*Check Flaws page 21 for ideas, pick no more than 2*)

What are their quirks?_____
(*Check Quirks Page 20 for ideas, pick no more than 2*)

Where do they live?_____

What do they do?_____

What do they love? _____

List things they hate: _____

List things they are good at: _____

List things they are bad at: _____

CHARACTER SHEET

What is their family like? _____

_____

_____

_____

_____

_____

_____

_____

_____

_____

What is their backstory? _____

_____

_____

_____

_____

_____

_____

_____

_____

_____

_____

_____

CHARACTER SHEET

Draw or tape character
inspiration here.

First Name:_____

Last Name: _____

Physical Description: _____

_____

_____

_____

Age: _____

What does this character *want*? _____

What does this character *need*?_____

What are their flaws?_____
(*Check Flaws page 21 for ideas, pick no more than 2*)

What are their quirks?_____
(*Check Quirks Page 20 for ideas, pick no more than 2*)

Where do they live?_____

What do they do?_____

What do they love? _____

List things they hate: _____

List things they are good at: _____

List things they are bad at: _____

CHARACTER SHEET

What is their family like? _____

_____

_____

_____

_____

_____

_____

_____

What is their backstory? _____

_____

_____

_____

_____

_____

_____

_____

_____

_____

_____

WHERE IS YOUR STORY?

Sometimes our stories have more than one **setting**. Use these pages to fill as little or as many setting details you need.

Where is your story primarily set? _____
(Outer space, Washington State, fantasy forest, under water.)

Name of your world: *(Could be real or made up.)*
_____

What is the time period(s)?_____

_____

_____

_____

Where does this part of your story start?

_____

_____

_____

Describe the landscape: _____

_____

_____

_____

_____

_____

_____

WHERE IS YOUR STORY?

What is the government system like? (*It can be real or made up.*)

_____

_____

_____

_____

_____

Who is in charge? (*A president, a king, a queen, etc.*)

_____

What are some of the big rules people have to follow in your setting?

_____

_____

_____

_____

What currency do they use? (*dollars, coins, stardust, etc.*) _____

Additional setting notes:

_____

_____

_____

_____

WHERE IS YOUR STORY?

Sometimes our stories have more than one **setting**. Use these pages to fill as little or as many setting details you need.

Where is your story primarily set? _____

(Outer space, Washington State, fantasy forest, under water.)

Name of your world: *(Could be real or made up.)*

_____

What is the time period(s)?_____

_____

_____

_____

Where does this part of your story start?

_____

_____

_____

Describe the landscape: _____

_____

_____

_____

_____

_____

_____

WHERE IS YOUR STORY?

What is the government system like? (*It can be real or made up.*)

_____

_____

_____

_____

_____

Who is in charge? (*A president, a king, a queen, etc.*)

_____

What are some of the big rules people have to follow in your setting?

_____

_____

_____

_____

What currency do they use? (*dollars, coins, stardust, etc.*) _____

Additional setting notes:

_____

_____

_____

_____

WHERE IS YOUR STORY?

Sometimes our stories have more than one **setting**. Use these pages to fill as little or as many setting details you need.

Where is your story primarily set? _____

(Outer space, Washington State, fantasy forest, under water.)

Name of your world: *(Could be real or made up.)*
_____

What is the time period(s)?_____

_____

_____

_____

Where does this part of your story start?

_____

_____

_____

Describe the landscape: _____

_____

_____

_____

_____

_____

_____

WHERE IS YOUR STORY?

What is the government system like? (*It can be real or made up.*)

_____

_____

_____

_____

_____

Who is in charge? (*A president, a king, a queen, etc.*)

_____

What are some of the big rules people have to follow in your setting?

_____

_____

_____

_____

What currency do they use? (*dollars, coins, stardust, etc.*) _____

Additional setting notes:

_____

_____

_____

_____

WHERE IS YOUR STORY?

Sometimes our stories have more than one **setting**. Use these pages to fill as little or as many setting details you need.

Where is your story primarily set? _____

(Outer space, Washington State, fantasy forest, under water.)

Name of your world: *(Could be real or made up.)*

_____

What is the time period(s)?_____

_____

_____

_____

Where does this part of your story start?

_____

_____

_____

Describe the landscape: _____

_____

_____

_____

_____

_____

_____

WHERE IS YOUR STORY?

What is the government system like? (*It can be real or made up*.)

_____

_____

_____

_____

_____

Who is in charge? (*A president, a king, a queen, etc.*)

_____

What are some of the big rules people have to follow in your setting?

_____

_____

_____

_____

What currency do they use? (*dollars, coins, stardust, etc.*) _____

Additional setting notes:

_____

_____

_____

_____

WHERE IS YOUR STORY?

Sometimes our stories have more than one **setting**. Use these pages to fill as little or as many setting details you need.

Where is your story primarily set? _____

(Outer space, Washington State, fantasy forest, under water.)

Name of your world: *(Could be real or made up.)*

_____

What is the time period(s)?_____

_____

_____

_____

Where does this part of your story start?

_____

_____

_____

Describe the landscape: _____

_____

_____

_____

_____

_____

_____

WHERE IS YOUR STORY?

What is the government system like? (*It can be real or made up.*)

_____

_____

_____

_____

Who is in charge? (*A president, a king, a queen, etc.*)

_____

What are some of the big rules people have to follow in your setting?

_____

_____

_____

What currency do they use? (*dollars, coins, stardust, etc.*) _____

Additional setting notes:

_____

_____

_____

_____

_____

Section 6:
INDEX

PUBLISHING PATHWAYS

The publishing world has changed a lot in the last decade. Today, there are more ways than ever to publish your books. In this section, we will explore three major pathways to getting published. Hopefully, this will help you decide what is the best fit for you.

The Big Five

There are five major publishing houses in the United States.

- Hachette Book Group
- HarperCollins
- Penguin Random House
- Macmillian Publishers
- Simon & Schuster

Each of these big publishing houses have multiple imprints focusing on different genres or markets. Typically, these publishing houses do not accept *unagented work*. Which means if you send them your manuscript directly, it's unlikely to be read. If you want your book published with the Big Five, you'll need a **literary agent.**

What is a literary agent?

A literary agent helps you pitch your book to publishers, negotiate contracts, and guides you through the complex world of book publishing. Think of them as your partner! They represent you and your book.

How do you find an agent?

- **The Writer's Market:** This annually updated guide lists literary agencies and publishers. Use it to find out if an agency represents your type of book. Browse their agents online for what their preferences are. Each agent will have a wish list of what they want. Pay close attention to those lists!
- **Writing Conferences:** Many conferences offer opportunities to pitch your work directly to agents.
- **Publishers Marketplace:** This website connects writers, agents, editors, and publishers.

What is a query letter?

To get an agent you will need to send them a **query letter**. A query letter is a short, professional email that introduces your book. It should highlight your story's stakes in an engaging way—it's what will hook the agent. There are so many guides or sample letters online. Study them! Agents are not shy about what they like to see in a query. Listen to them! Especially, those you may want to pitch to.

PUBLISHING PATHWAYS

Small Press/Independent Presses

Not all publishing houses require an agent. Some small presses accept direct submissions. Which means you can pitch your manuscript without an agent.

What are small presses?

Small presses are publishers that make less than $50 million dollars a year. Many focus on certain niche genres and regional markets. They publish fewer books a year----sometimes less than ten!

Why consider a small press?

Small presses often have a more personal relationship with their authors. They work closely to help refine and prepare your book for publication. However, they do have less resources for marketing and distribution than larger publishers.

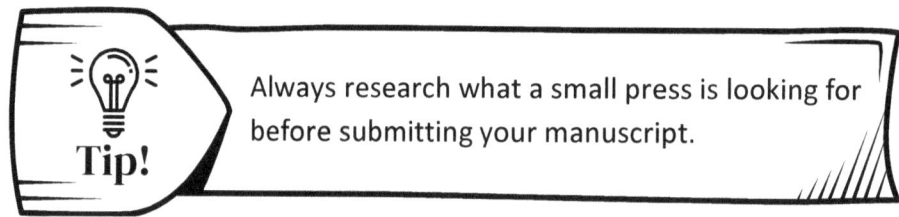

Tip! Always research what a small press is looking for before submitting your manuscript.

Independent Publishing/Self-Publishing

In this pathway, you are the publisher. You have complete creative control but you are then responsible for every aspect of the publishing process including:

- Editing
- Formatting
- Cover design
- Marketing and public relations
- Taxes and business administration

Sounds like a lot I know! But there are many reasons people choose this pathway.

Why chose indie publishing?

1. **Sharing your story with family and friends** – You don't care about bookstores' shelves or big promotions. Maybe you just want to see it printed and share it with loved ones.
2. **Your book doesn't follow market trends** – Publishing houses are businesses and as such they will only contract books they feel are trending in the market. If your book doesn't fit a publisher's current list, maybe you publish it yourself!
3. **You are a businessperson** – You have a clear marketing plan, you know your target audience, you want to keep the profits to yourself.
4. **You want all the creative freedom** – You control the timeline for when your book is published, you get to decide the cover, the length, the look and feel. If this is something you need in the publishing process, then this pathway gives you all that flexibility.

TERMS & DEFINITIONS

TERM	DEFINITION	PAGE
ACTIVE VOICE	Writing that tells us what a person is doing.	61-62
ANTAGONIST	The one that is in opposition.	38
ARCS	The story structure and/or character's progression.	30
AUTHORIAL	A writer's personal style. How they write.	61
CENTRAL MESSAGE	The issue or idea in your theme.	28
CHAPTER	Used to divide a book into sections.	47
CHARACTER	A person in a story.	6, 9-22, 30
CLIMAX	The most exciting part of a story.	41, 44
COMPOUND WORDS	Words that have two or more words put together.	88
CONFLICT	A disagreement. When things fight against each other or oppose one another.	41
CONTRAST	The difference between two things.	38
CRISIS	Intense danger or trouble.	41
DESCRIPTIVE	To describe something. Show in words what something is.	63-64
DIALOGUE	Characters talking	63-72
DIALOGUE TAGS	Words that appear before, after, or at the end of dialogue to tell us who is speaking and/or how they spoke.	63-72
ERA	A time period.	23, 69
FANTASY	A story about fictional worlds that are not real.	81
FICTION	Something that is not real. It is made up.	81
FLASHBACK	Scenes that happen out of chronological order.	87
FORESHADOWING	Hints in our stories for future events or messages.	28

TERMS & DEFINITIONS

TERM	DEFINITION	PAGE
GENRE	A category of writing.	81-82
HYPHEN	A short dash (-) that is used to join words in specific situations.	88
IMAGERY	Using words to call on a reader's senses	73-74
INCIDENT	An event.	35
INCITING	To incite, encourage, or persuade.	35
INSURMOUNTABLE	Overwhelming, unconquerable.	6
LIMITED	The reader only knows what one character at a time knows.	56
MAIMING	To be injured.	7
MANNERISM	The way something speaks or behaves.	20
NARRATIVE	A story.	30, 60
NARRATION	Act of telling a story.	58, 60-61, 70
NARRATOR	A storyteller.	59, 60
NOVEL	A long fictional story.	1, 83
OMNISCIENT	The narrator knows everything.	59
PACING	Completing something at a steady rate.	67-68
PASSIVE	Writing that tells us what is being done to the person or thing.	61-62
PERSPECTIVE	Perspective is how someone sees their world.	58-60, 80

TERMS & DEFINITIONS

TERM	DEFINITION	PAGE
PLOT	The events that show us how your character solves their problem.	6, 29, 32, 33
POV	Point of view. POV is the method for narration: first person, second person, or third person.	58-60
PROBLEM	An issue that your character needs to solve.	6-8
PROTAGONIST	The main character in a story.	6
RELATABILITY	Seeing yourself in someone's story.	9
REVERSAL	When the character comes close to achieving their first goal, only to realize what they wanted may not be what they needed.	40
SCENE	A section of continuous story.	34-46
SETTING	The time and place the story happens.	23-27
STAKES	What happens if your character doesn't follow through with their journey.	37
STYLE	The way in which a author writes their story.	61-62
SUBGENRE	A smaller categorical genre or genre within a genre.	81-82
TENSION	The way you create a sense of anticipation for the reader.	75
THEME	The central message or main idea of a story.	28-29
TONE	The mood in which the character said it. The mood in which author wrote it.	62-65
VOICE	The unique attitude and style in which an author writes.	61-62

THINGS I WISH I KNEW!

Our final notes of encouragement and advice for you.

Brittany Tucker: I wish I'd known it was okay to fail. That losing is a brilliant way to learn. That I didn't need to fit within anyone's expectations for me—I am the boss of that. That being weird isn't weird. I was given this amazing, whimsical, wild mind for a reason. I am not a mistake. Neither are you.

Remember that. Those whacky worlds in your head are beautiful.

Brittany Padgett: I wish I'd known that my itch to write would never go away. That I'd feel most like myself when I was writing. True passion doesn't fade, instead it brings joy and peace, even when the road is hard. Writing takes time and hard work, but because I love it so much, it feels like it's exactly where I'm meant to be.

You'll never stop learning. The more we learn, the more we realize how much more there is to know. Take every opportunity to grow. Meet other writers—trust us, we're some of the most interesting and supportive people out there.

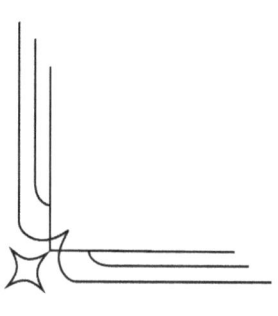

ABOUT THE AUTHORS

Brittany Tucker lives on an island off the coast of Washington state with her husband, daughter, a menagerie of furry and scaled children, and her imagination. She prefers generic cereal, collects tattoos and action figures, and was in the top 5% on the planet for ships sunk in Assassin's Creed III. She is a published author of over four fantasy novels (and counting).

Brittany Padgett is a young adult and children's author in the Pacific Northwest. Before pursuing her passion for writing and storytelling, she worked for ten years as a student affairs professional in higher education. She graduated with a bachelor's degree in English from Central Washington University. She was editor-in-chief at Manastash Literary Journal and business manager for Poetry Northwest. Brittany is best known for her middle-grade book series *The Reeds of West Hills*.